The Gallery opens 9.30—6.0

David Cross Gallery

3a Boyces Avenue, Clifton, Bristol. Telephone 32614

Specialists in Bristol and West Country
Paintings, Drawings, Prints,
Period and Modern Marines,
Landscapes and Watercolours,
Framing and Restoration

VIEW of CLIFTON and the HOT-WELLS.

After Rowbotham   c. 1830

1

The Clifton Guide

Michael Pascoe

REDCLIFFE PRESS (PUBLICATIONS) LTD.
14 DOWRY SQUARE, BRISTOL 8

Avenue of pleached limes, from The Fosseway

Contents

Credits

Cover illustration: View on the Avon at Hotwell, Samuel Jackson, c. 1832, reproduced by courtesy of Bristol City Art Gallery. *Photographs:* Cedric Barker. *Line drawings:* Frank Shipsides (reproduced from *Bristol: Profile of a City,* published by Redcliffe Press). *The map* on page 56 is reproduced by kind permission of Geographers' A-Z Company Ltd, and based upon the Ordnance Survey Map with the sanction of the Controller of Her Majesty's Stationery Office, Crown Copyright reserved.

ISBN 0 905459 26 1

© Michael Pascoe

Printed in Great Britain by Burleigh Ltd., Bristol

Brunel's great Suspension Bridge spanning the Avon

Foreword

It has been said that Clifton is an atmosphere, not just a place, and it is certainly true that there are some areas just beyond the boundaries of the parish which are Clifton in spirit. However, this Guide confines itself to the ancient limits of the parish of Clifton.

Every walk around Clifton and the Hotwells has its own charm and brings new discoveries to residents and visitors alike. No attempt has been made to prescribe any given route, but rather to let visitors make their own discoveries, referring to this Guide as and when they wish.

No guide book to Clifton has been published for at least sixty years. The increasing number of tourists visiting Clifton and the growing interest in local history have produced a demand which it is hoped that this booklet will meet.

M.J.P.

Clifton—past and present

The earliest inhabitants of Clifton, Anglo-Saxon for 'the inhabited place on the cliff', left their mark on Observatory Hill where remains of an Iron Age camp can still be traced. This superb defensive site was also used by the Romans. A ford crossed the River Avon under the present Suspension Bridge until demolished as a danger to shipping in the late 19th century.

After this, little is known of Clifton's history until the Royal manor of Clifton is described in the Domesday Book, a survey of his kingdom ordered by William the Conqueror in 1085. The population at this time was about thirty.

One hundred and fifty years later the manor passed to William de Clifton and then through several owners until in the 16th century it was divided into two, the smaller manor going to the Chief Falconer of Queen Elizabeth I. After the Civil War, in which Clifton was burnt by the Royalists, the Bristol merchants' guild, the Society of Merchant Venturers, bought and reunited the two manors in 1686. At the beginning of the 18th century Clifton was still a small rural community of fewer than three hundred people, mainly farmworkers, living in small houses clustered around St Andrew's Church on Clifton Green or at the foot of the hill.

About this time the Merchant Venturers began to appreciate the potential value of the hot spring not far from the foot of the present Suspension Bridge which was attracting a growing number of visitors. The Merchant Venturers built the first Pump House and the Hotwell quickly developed into a popular spa, frequented by fashionable society until the end of the 18th century.

At the same time, a handful of prosperous merchants began to move out from crowded Bristol to Clifton on the hill, building mansions in their own grounds around the church.

It was not until the national building boom of the mid 1780s that most of Clifton's fine Georgian terraces were built. During these few years about twenty major terraces were laid out, transforming a small Gloucestershire village into a thriving urban community. In 1793, with the outbreak of the Napoleonic Wars, came a sudden slump. Developers were ruined overnight and many of the terraces were not completed until the early years of the 19th century.

Francis Greenway's Assembly Rooms

The popularity of the Hotwell had by now declined but, under the control of the Merchant Venturers acting as a planning authority, Clifton's development as a popular suburb for the well-to-do was assured. The 19th century saw the building of Regency villas, the mansions of the Promenade, and more terraces, often of a better architectural standard than those of the 18th century. Rows of Victorian residences extended north towards the Downs and eastwards to Whiteladies Road. In 1835 Clifton became part of the City and County of Bristol.

Although many of Clifton's larger terrace houses were used as lodging houses, private hotels and schools, a substantial number were occupied by families. The number of residents increased steadily from 8,000 in 1821, doubling by 1851 and reaching 29,000 in 1891. The opening of Clifton College in 1860, Clifton High School for Girls in 1877 and the increasing facilities of the City on the doorstep all helped to attract and retain residents.

After the First World War the sense of community was somewhat weakened by the exodus of many wealthier residents to the countryside. Smaller families and the disappearance of servants saw many more Clifton houses converted into flats and bedsitters, usually without imagination and often involving the destruction of original features.

Bomb damage during the Second World War, the post-war scarcity of building materials, absentee landlords, planners' blight and neglect by the local authority which still assumed that Clifton was able to look after itself, all took their toll and reduced the area to a low ebb.

In the last twenty years Clifton has seen something of a rebirth. Throughout the country popular appreciation of our Georgian and Victorian heritage has increased and the attractiveness and convenience of Clifton has led to more houses being bought for owner-occupation or for sensitive conversion into flats which are then sold to caring owners.

Today the phrase 'Clifton Village' is often used to describe the heart of Clifton. It has been dismissed as an estate agent's term, but there is more than a grain of truth in the description. The community spirit has returned. Local residents' societies are steadily improving houses and gardens and have joined together in several projects, including the enormously successful Clifton Village Fayres of 1978 and 1979 and 'Clifton in Bloom'. In 1980, as well as these events, Clifton is launching its own ten-day

Festival to coincide with and complement Bristol's International Wine Fair.

There is still much to be done to restore, improve and protect Clifton and especially Hotwells. Residents are fortunate in having a vigilant Clifton and Hotwells Improvement Society, the largest amenity society in Bristol, and many smaller groups have completed self-help schemes aided by the Society. A more enlightened approach by the local authority and in particular the Town Scheme Grants made available by the Department of the Environment have also produced dramatic improvements in recent years.

The Avon Gorge

The three hundred foot chasm of the Avon Gorge has for long drawn visitors to it. During the 18th century it formed an added attraction for those visiting the Hotwell and its scenery appealed to writers and artists of the Romantic movement in the late 18th and early 19th centuries. Its craggy, sinuous beauty may be an attraction to the visitor but to the sailor its twists and turns and wind currents presented considerable difficulties in navigation. The rise and fall of the tide is amongst the highest in the world and in the days of sail, ships were normally towed up the channel by rowing boats. The evolution of steam and larger ships produced several spectacular wrecks in the Gorge and new docks were eventually constructed at Avonmouth at the end of the 19th century.

The rocks on the Clifton side of the Gorge are named after St Vincent. In medieval times there was a chapel dedicated to this Spanish saint who was martyred in AD 305. No trace of the chapel now remains.

Before the development of the science of geology, the formation of the Gorge remained a puzzle to our ancestors.

The most colourful explanation produced was that it was the work of two giant brothers, the hard-working Vincent and the lazy Goram. Vincent suggested to Goram that to achieve ever-lasting fame they should dig a ravine and divert the course of the Avon. Vincent set to work while Goram watched but was

eventually shamed into working and decided to cut a rival channel across the Downs.

The giants had only one pickaxe between them so they threw it to each other, the distance being only three miles! One day Goram dropped off to sleep and failed to hear his brother's warning shout as he threw the pickaxe. It hit him on the head, killing him instantly. Although full of sorrow, Vincent completed his task and, while admiring it, accidentally slipped, fell into the Gorge and was swept out to sea by the full tide.

Geologists now believe that the Gorge was formed during the Ice Age, up to one million years ago. It is thought that ice coming down from South Wales reached as far as Failand on the Somerset side of the Gorge and blocked the normal outflow of the river. The river cut back and eroded its way through the limestone cliffs. This limestone is about 270 million years old, and was originally laid down in the sea which explains the marine fossils which occur in it.

The rocks were quarried for centuries both for their stone and for the high quality lime they produce. Many of the scars produced by these quarries are still visible. The rocks also contain quartz crystals, in the form of geodes, which are called 'Bristol Diamonds'. These were polished and sold to visitors to the Hotwell and are indistinguishable to the layman from genuine diamonds.

Today occasional falls of rock onto the Portway beneath have perturbed the local authority. A covered tunnel is at present being built which will protect the Portway from tumbling rocks.

The Gorge has long been renowned for its flora and as early as 1562 the first rare plant was recorded by a local clergyman.

At least thirty different rare and uncommon plants grow in the Gorge. Of these, three are unknown elsewhere in the world: the Bristol Whitebeam (*Sorbus bristoliensis*), Wilmott's Whitebeam (*Sorbus wilmottiana*) and a hybrid orchid.

Other plants grow in the Gorge and its environs but not elsewhere in mainland Britain such as the Bristol rock cress (*Arabis scabra*) and the round-headed leek or Bristol onion (*Allium sphaerocephalom*).

At the end of the last century a Clifton schoolmaster threw keeled garlic (*Allium carinatum*) into the Gorge. This alien has spread so much that it has exterminated some rare plants and threatens others. An even greater danger is the human species which each year picks these rare flowers. This is illegal and anti-social. Flowers are the reproductive part of plants and if they are picked the survival of the species is endangered and a legacy for future generations is destroyed.

At the foot of the Gorge on the Leigh Woods side is the railway line of the Bristol and Portishead Pier and Railway Company formed in 1863 to link Portishead dock with the City. A rival line, the Bristol Port Railway and Pier, linking Hotwells with Avonmouth opened on the Clifton bank two years later. The Portway, the main road to Avonmouth, was constructed this century.

Opposite Clifton lies the beautiful Nightingale Valley and Leigh Woods, part of which is National Trust property and has several popular Nature Trails.

The Clifton Suspension Bridge

In 1753, a wealthy Bristol wine merchant, William Vick, left in his will £1000 to the Society of Merchant Venturers with instructions that the sum should be invested until it reached £10,000 when it should be used for building a stone bridge from Clifton Down to Leigh Woods.

By 1829 the bequest had reached £8,000 and with Thomas Telford's Menai Straits Bridge in the news, a Committee was formed to carry out Vick's plan.

The cost of a stone bridge was estimated to be at least £60,000 and it was decided to apply to Parliament for permission to build an iron structure, additional funds to be raised by loans, gifts and tolls.

Designs were invited and Telford was appointed judge. Isambard Kingdom Brunel, then aged twenty-three, submitted four designs. To the consternation of the Committee, Telford rejected all the designs, putting forward one of his own which was expensive and thought ugly by many people. This comprised two hollow Gothic piers rising from the foot of the Gorge carrying a centre span of 400 feet.

The lack of funds gave the Committee an excuse to hold a new competition. Brunel's design was placed second, but after meeting

Clifton College, dating from the 1860s

with the judges and trustees, Brunel so impressed them that not only was his design accepted but he was also appointed engineer for the project. This design had towers in the style of ancient Egyptian architecture, surmounted by sphinxes. Scenes depicting the building of the bridge formed bas reliefs on the sides of the towers.

The first turf was cut in 1831, but the Bristol Riots of the same year and an economic recession severely affected the flow of funds and work was abandoned.

The Egyptian ornamentation was scrapped to save costs and in 1836 construction started again with the piers. First, an iron bar 800 feet long was placed across the Gorge with a basket slung below for moving materials. Brunel and a boy were the first to cross and this became so popular that the trustees were able to charge five shillings (25p) a trip.

By 1840 the core of the huge piers was complete and orders were placed for the ironwork. By 1843 it was announced that £40,000 had been spent and that £30,000 more would be needed. Funds again dried up, work stopped, and in 1853 the ironwork and plant were sold. Brunel died of overwork six years later.

A short time after Brunel's death the Institution of Civil Engineers decided to complete the Clifton Bridge as a memorial to him. The Hungerford Suspension Bridge in London, built by Brunel some years earlier, was to be replaced by a railway bridge and the Hungerford chains were available. The money was quickly raised and the Hungerford chains bought. Brunel's design was slightly modified, three chains were used instead of two, the anchor chains brought closer to the bridge and the roadway widened by six feet. In 1862 work began again. Wire ropes were placed across the piers and planks laid on top. Another rope with a travelling hoist was placed above so that materials could be shifted. The chains were put together link by link on this platform, followed by the roadway girders.

The opening was performed jointly by the Lords Lieutenant of Somerset and Gloucestershire on December 8th 1864. Thousands of spectators watched a mile-long procession and a vast Victorian banquet was held for important guests.

The bridge is 245 feet above the Portway, measures 1,352 feet from anchorage to anchorage, and 702 feet between the piers. The piers are 86 feet high and the chains weigh 1,100 tons.

These bare statistics do not reveal Brunel's technical genius

which has given the bridge a place in engineering history. His original design of two lines of two chains and his method of connecting the suspension rods to both chains, thus spreading the load, were innovations which added to the aesthetic effect while reducing cost and weight. Similarly, the use of horizontal roller beds rather than arches for the chains reduced stress on the towers. Perhaps Brunel's attention to detail is best exemplified by the fact that the Leigh Woods side of the bridge is three feet lower than the Clifton side, thus avoiding the optical illusion of a slope which the different rock profiles would give to a horizontal bridge.

Once completed, the bridge enabled the far side of the Gorge to be developed for residential use. Local residents quickly formed the Leigh Woods Land Company to prevent wholesale development which would have destroyed the scenery. Today the bridge provides a valuable link to the 800 acres of Ashton Court, a public open space, and a route to the beautiful countryside surrounding Bristol.

Amongst the many Bristol stories which are told is that of Sarah Ann Henley who is said to have thrown herself off the bridge in 1885 after being crossed in love. It is reputed that her crinoline acted as a parachute and she was rescued, uninjured, from the river bank and lived on into old age.

The bridge is administered by the Clifton Suspension Bridge Trust and day-to-day running is in charge of a Bridge Inspector who supervises the toll collectors and the permanent maintenance staff.

The Observatory

In 1828 William West, an artist of the Bristol School and amateur scientist, leased from the Society of Merchant Venturers a ruined windmill which had stood empty for sixty years on what is now Observatory Hill. A strong gale in 1778 had driven the sails so fast that the wooden pivots had caught fire and the mill had burnt down, a bare two years after its construction.

West rebuilt the ruin with a telescope on top of the tower, replacing it later by his first camera obscura. (A camera obscura

The Observatory

is a lens fitted into a revolving cowling on the roof. The lens acts like a camera, picking up the view in all directions and reflecting it by a mirror on to a large shallow white saucer-shaped table situated in a darkened room. Viewers around the table can see all the movement and colour caught by the lens and reflected in miniature.) West went on to extend the building to house a variety of astronomical instruments and also constructed a revolving observatory.

While installing equipment to look upwards, West was also making progress downwards. In 1837, after two years of tunnelling, a 200 foot long passage was completed running from the Observatory to the 'Giant's Cave', some ninety feet below in the face of St Vincent's Rocks. The cave was reputed to have been a hermit's cell in the Middle Ages. By 1839 West was advertising 'various kinds of photogenic drawing' and 'superior photogenic paper' for sale. This was a form of sensitised paper on which an image could be produced.

William West died in 1861, but his descendants continued to live in the Observatory until 1943. After the Second World War the Observatory and Cave were again opened to the public. In 1977 the Society of Merchant Venturers sold the Observatory. After two years of neglect it again changed hands and is being restored.

The Hotwells

At the foot of St Vincent's Rocks in the Gorge, under the present Suspension Bridge, a spring of warm water formerly bubbled through the mud, at a rate of sixty gallons a minute and at a temperature of 76°F. Although twenty-six feet below the river at high tide, at low tide it was ten feet above the water level.

This spring is mentioned in a 15th century account of Clifton as being used by sailors suffering from scurvy and had a steady usage, mainly by local residents.

In 1677 Catherine of Braganza, Charles II's Queen, visited the well and the Society of Merchant Venturers later acquired the spring when they became lords of the manor of Clifton. In 1695 they leased the well for ninety years at a nominal rent on

Open Monday—Saturday 12.30—2.30 p.m. 7.00—12.00 p.m.

ROSSI'S
35 Princess Victoria Street, Clifton, Bristol.
Tel: 30049 (Advisable to make reservation)

Warm intimate atmosphere. Signore Rossi personally cooks and supervises the kitchen.
Meet your friends and relax in our comfortable upstairs lounge before or after your meal.

Tiziano
fashions

Beautiful clothes and accessories
for all occasions

54 The Mall, Clifton, Bristol 8
Telephone 30240

condition that a pump room and other amenities were built. The Hotwell House was built in the following year and a pump installed to raise the water with valves which, in theory, would shut against river pollution at high tide. In practice, however, this was not successful and pollution by the river water often occurred.

The rise of the Hotwell was meteoric and newspapers regularly reported arrivals of the aristocracy and gentry. The Duke of York, the Duchess of Marlborough and the Prince of Orange were amongst the visitors and the Earl of Jersey gave a breakfast party for 150 people.

The Bristol Hotwell complemented the Bath spa; the season being from April to September, whereas Bath was predominantly a winter resort. Not the least of the Hotwell's attractions was its cheapness, a room costing ten shillings (50p) a week, servants half price.

As the Hotwell developed in popularity, the facilities increased. Two assembly rooms were built near the end of Dowry Parade and offered breakfasts and dances, as well as more formal balls under the supervision of a Master of Ceremonies. Pleasure gardens, a small theatre on Jacob's Wells Road and a colonnade of shops next to the Pump House all enticed visitors. Fashionable visitors' were also attracted by the awe-inspiring Gorge, rides and drives up to the Downs and boat trips with strawberry teas at Ashton across the river or accompanied by musicians for whom the Gorge formed a natural echo chamber.

As well as those who came for pleasure, there were invalids and attendant hordes of physicians who claimed that the waters were efficacious in curing diseases as wide-ranging as 'hot livers', 'feeble brains', 'old sores' and diabetes. It was as a cure for consumption that the spa was most famous. The water was not only drunk on the spot; a thriving export trade both in Britain and in Europe helped to support Bristol's glass-making industry. Attempts were made to exploit other natural springs in different parts of Clifton and Hotwells but without success.

If the rise of the Hotwell was meteoric, its decline was no less swift. When the ninety year lease expired in 1785, the Society of Merchant Venturers required over £1,500, a large sum at that period, to be spent on the quay, the pump and general improvements. At first the Society failed to find a tenant and carried out the work themselves, later leasing the Hotwell at a greatly increased rent. The lessee in turn was forced to raise prices from ten shillings (50p) a season per family to twenty-six shillings (£1.30) per month per person. This had the effect of driving away those in pursuit of pleasure and the spa was soon frequented almost entirely by incurable invalids whose high mortality rate did nothing to enhance the Hotwell's reputation. Many of them are buried in the Strangers' Burial Ground on Clifton Hill. The economic slump during the Napoleonic Wars and the freedom of the wealthy to travel abroad again after Napoleon's defeat in 1815 caused a further decline in the fortunes of the Hotwell.

During the declining years of the spa Dr Thomas Beddoes arrived in Clifton from Oxford where he had been Reader in Chemistry at the University. Beddoes had already done research into the medical use of airs and gases and felt that the Hotwell would provide the tubercular patients he needed for his practical experiments. He set up a 'Pneumatic Institution' first in Hope Square, later transferring to Dowry Square, and helped by wealthy friends such as Thomas Wedgwood.

Although Beddoes was sceptical of the virtues of Hotwell water, some of his own experiments were not entirely conventional. Amongst them was a theory that cows' breath could help consumption and landladies were cajoled into allowing cows to be tethered in bedrooms with their heads through the bed curtains!

The Pneumatic Institution closed in 1801 and its main claim to fame lies in the fact that Beddoes engaged as an assistant a young Cornishman, Humphry Davy, later to achieve national fame for his experiments into electricity and for the invention of the miner's safety lamp. During their time at Dowry Square, Davy and Beddoes conducted experiments into the properties of laughing gas or nitrous oxide, the basis of modern anaesthesia.

Two further major attempts were made to revive the spa. The old Hotwell House was demolished in 1822 to facilitate the building of Bridge Valley Road and a new and improved Pump Room built to replace it. In spite of some energetic salesmanship by at least one proprietor, the enterprise was a failure and the building was demolished in 1867. This allowed the removal of Hotwell Point, a promontory dangerous to shipping. The spring was enclosed and piped through to a small cavern hollowed in the rock and served from a pump until 1913, when pollution was so evident that it was closed by the authorities on health grounds. The cavern still exists alongside the busy Portway.

Sion Hill

25

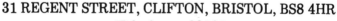

A final effort to re-establish a spa took place at the end of the 19th century. In 1890 Sir George Newnes, the publisher, applied to the Merchant Venturers for permission to build a cliff railway to link Hotwell Road tramway terminal with Sion Hill. The Society agreed on condition that Sir George built a hydropathic institution and pump room. This opened as the Clifton Grand Spa Hydro in 1898, later becoming the present Avon Gorge Hotel. The Rocks Railway closed before the Second World War, during which the tunnel was used by the BBC as air-raid proof studios. The entrances to the Rocks Railway can be seen beside the Avon Gorge Hotel and on the Portway.

All that now remains of the Hotwell's former glory is part of the Colonnade on the Portway, past which thousands of vehicles thunder each day.

Bristol Zoo

The Zoo, or to give it its full title, the Bristol, Clifton and West of England Zoological Society, was set up in Clifton in September, 1835, to promote zoology, arboriculture and horticulture. Two hundred and twenty subscribers, amongst them I. K. Brunel, and both W. D. and H. O. Wills, bought shares at £25 each. The Society was, and still is, non-profit making and pays no dividends.

The Zoo was officially opened on July 11th 1836 with the landscaping of the gardens still incomplete, and only a small stock of animals, some contributed by sea captains and West Indies merchants.

The Society was set up as a scientific institution devoted to popular culture, two contrasting aims which did not entirely mix. Much of the income was derived from fetes (often with fireworks), concerts, croquet and archery tournaments. These attractions were first thought of as temporary expedients but later developed into permanent features during the first hundred years of the Zoo's life. Sunday opening to the public and the sale of alcohol were not allowed by the shareholders.

Clifton expanded steadily through the 19th century and the Bank Holiday Acts, the foundation of Clifton College and Clifton

High School for Girls all helped to improve the financial position, although there was still a great reliance on fetes.

During the First World War, the Zoo 'did its bit'. It provided the Admiralty with a seal which scientists thought might be trained to detect and warn against enemy submarines. The experiment was a failure.

By the early 1920s the Zoo was at a low ebb. The gardens were still Victorian in appearance, and although the Zoo was now open to the general public on Sundays, visitors were not being attracted. New blood on the Committee in the mid-twenties reversed the trend. The monkey temple was built in 1927, the gardens were modernised and improved, a restaurant with private ballroom opened in 1930 and many new animals were bought or reared, Bristol being the first zoo in Europe to breed a chimpanzee in 1934. The attractive frieze of animals above the entrance dates from 1929.

In 1938, for the first time in the Zoo's history, there was no income from fetes; the new improvements and additions made them unnecessary and the Zoo was at last fulfilling its original aims.

The outbreak of the Second World War with the possibility of air raids meant that certain dangerous animals had to be put down, or, in more fortunate cases, evacuated to zoos in areas less likely to be targets for enemy bombs. In the event, only one high explosive bomb fell on the Zoo, killing a deer. Incendiary bombs also fell but did not cause serious damage. The flower gardens were converted into vegetable plots, but the number of visitors rose, amongst them Queen Mary, then staying at Badminton, and American soldiers from General Omar Bradley's staff, based at Clifton College.

In 1948 Alfred the gorilla died of tuberculosis at the age of twenty-one. Alfred had been bought during the pre-war re-stocking and was a star in his own right and as much a sight for visitors to the City as Clifton Suspension Bridge. Now he stands preserved in the city Museum and his bust in stone is at the entrance to the new ape house.

The links first formed with the University of Bristol in the 1930s began to pay dividends and the Zoo not only acquired new animals but began to enhance its reputation as a centre for breeding endangered species. The 1950s saw a bear pit, wading birds' enclosure and an outdoor aviary built, plus greenhouses, potting sheds, laboratories, animals' hospital and food preparation rooms.

In July 1961 Rosie, the Zoo's popular elephant, died. She had been at the Zoo since 1938 and gave 80,000 rides to children every year.

The 1960s saw the arrival of a pair of okapis from the strife-torn Congo, their only habitat, and a pair of white tigers, the only ones except for Washington Zoo outside India. Both the okapis and the white tigers have bred several times and the Zoo continues to breed many species including giraffes, black rhinoceros, polar bears and the first gorilla bred in Britain.

In 1966 the Zoo acquired the 190 acre Hollywood Tower Estate outside Bristol which is a haven for breeding endangered species and for growing horticultural produce.

The 1970s saw constant rebuilding with a new ape house, cat enclosure and animal hospital.

Today the well laid out and landscaped gardens and more than a thousand fishes, amphibians, reptiles, birds and mammals combine to attract over 600,000 visitors each year. The Zoo also continues to make significant contributions to research. Co-operation with other zoos has grown steadily and in 1978 Bristol Zoo took over Dudley Zoo. During the summer of 1980 a new reptile house and a modern nocturnal house will be opened.

Zoo information

Open every day except Christmas Day.
Mon–Sat from 9.00 a.m.
Sunday from 10.00 a.m.

Closing times vary according to the season, from 5.00 to 7.00 p.m.

Feeding times: Penguins 12.30 p.m.; lions and tigers 3.00 p.m.; sea lions 3.30 p.m.

A restaurant and bar operate throughout the year, and a cafeteria during the summer. The souvenir shop has work project sheets for school parties.

Telephone: Bristol 38951.

The Downs

In the Middle Ages Clifton and the adjoining Durdham Down were the grazing lands of the manor of Clifton and the neighbouring manor of Henbury. Boundary stones still exist in places across the Downs marking the limits of each manor.

During the Civil War between King and Parliament in the mid-17th century, Bristol changed hands twice. In 1643 Prince Rupert drew up his Royalist forces on the Downs in preparation for an attack on the city which had declared for Parliament. Much of the credit for the successful seizure of Bristol is due to Colonel Henry Washington (an ancestor of George Washington) whose daring cavalry charge breached the Parliamentary defences near the present City Museum in Queen's Road.

Two years later, as Parliamentary forces advanced on Bristol, Prince Rupert burnt much of Clifton to prevent Cromwell's army finding food and shelter. These efforts were in vain, and a beaten Prince Rupert was later allowed to withdraw with his army across the Downs.

With the rise of the Hotwells in the 18th century, the Downs became the playground of visitors. Riding up to the Downs was a favourite amusement, and fairs, horse racing and cricket were common. Gentlemen could also enjoy prize fights, bull-baiting, wrestling, cock-fighting or watching the lower orders attempt to catch a pig with a greased tail. Duels were also fought on the Downs, the last being recorded as late as 1837.

When deserted by the crowds, the Downs could be a dangerous place. Highwaymen and footpads lurked in the thick undergrowth, and even the gibbet with the skeletons of criminals hanging in chains, which stood at the north end of Gallows Acre Lane, now Pembroke Road, did not seem to deter thieves.

In the 19th century the Downs were in grave danger of disappearing. The common land was being gradually eaten away as houses were built, illegally enclosing parts of the Downs, and quarrying for building and road surfacing material and mining for lead, iron ore and other minerals scarred their appearance. Finally, by an Act of Parliament of 1861, the Society of Merchant Venturers, owners of the Clifton manor, gave Clifton Down to the people of Bristol, and Durdham Down was bought by the City for

£15,000 from the Lords of the manor of Henbury and given to the people of Bristol for ever.

On the former site of the Clifton Turnpike in Bridge Valley Road Alderman Proctor erected a Gothic drinking fountain as a gift to the people of Bristol to commemorate the acquisition of the Downs.

With the passing of the Downs Act the way was open for improvements. The scrubland was cleared, trees were planted, paths and roads laid out, quarries filled in and the Downs began to develop into the beautiful open space that we see today.

The 422 acres of the Downs are administered by the Downs Committee, drawn jointly from Merchant Venturers and City Councillors.

Artistic and Literary Clifton

Amongst those who flocked to the Hotwell were many of the famous literary and artistic figures of the 18th century including Addison, Defoe, Cowper, Pope, Gray, Sheridan, Haydn and Mrs Thrale, the friend of Dr Johnson.

Smollett's novel *Humphry Clinker* is partly set at the Hotwell. One of his characters, the sick Uncle Matthew, attacks the 'dirt, the stench, the chilling blasts and perpetual rains', but his niece, Lydia, loves the company, the views and the Downs and thinks the spa a 'charming romantic place'.

Fanny Burney set her novel *Evelina* entirely at the spa and the heroine enthuses over this 'most delightful spot; the prospect is beautiful, the air pure, and the weather very favourable to invalids'.

As the Georgian houses of central Clifton were completed and the Regency and Victorian development got under way, Clifton became less a resort for visitors and more the home of residents. The major figures did not flock to Clifton in the same way as in the previous century but they were replaced by large numbers of leisured people interested in the arts and acting as a counterbalance to a thriving commercial city.

Amongst the more famous of these residents were the poet Walter Savage Landor, Hannah More and John Addington

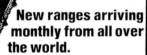 

Symonds, the historian of Renaissance Italy. Visitors included Southey, Coleridge, Maria Edgeworth, Macaulay and Carlyle.

The Mall Assembly Rooms were found to be inadequate and in 1841 the much more spacious Victoria Rooms were opened. As well as performances by local societies there were readings from his novels by Charles Dickens and concerts by Dame Clara Butt.

Gradually a cultural centre began to grow up on the fringe of Clifton in the Queen's Road area. In 1854 the Bristol Fine Arts Academy opposite the Victoria Rooms was opened. This fine building, partly altered in Edwardian times, has an Italianate facade designed by John Hirst and a Greek Revival interior by Charles Underwood. Now the Royal West of England Academy, it hosts several shows each year.

Sixteen years later, further along Queen's Road, the Bristol Museum and Library were housed in a Venetian Gothic building which owes much to Ruskin's teaching. The designers were John Foster and Archibald Ponton. Many of the decorative details were destroyed by enemy action in the Second World War and it now belongs to the University.

The founding of the University College in 1876 and the present City Museum and Art Gallery which opened in 1904 firmly established the area as a cultural centre.

The City Art Gallery contains many pictures by the Bristol School of Artists. Although not specifically Cliftonian, this group of amateur and professional artists which flourished in the 1820s, took the Avon Gorge and Leigh Woods as a favourite subject. Amongst the artists forming this school were Francis Danby, James Johnson, William West, Rolinda Sharples and Samuel Jackson. (A reproduction of a picture by Samuel Jackson forms the cover of this Guide.)

Clifton Cathedral

Places of Interest

There is such a wealth of interesting architecture in Clifton that it is impossible to describe every street, each building and all the famous residents. Listed in alphabetical order below are a few buildings and streets about which the visitor may wish to know more.

All Saints' Church, Pembroke Road

Designed by noted architect G. E. Street in 1868. Like Holy Trinity Church, Hotwells, it was gutted during the Second World War, enemy bombs destroying an excellent example of good Victorian church architecture. The interior was reconstructed after the War and contains striking fibre glass windows by John Piper.

Bishop's House, Clifton Hill

Originally known as the Church House, it is possible that this is the site of Clifton's manor house. The present mansion was built in the early 18th century and a wing added later. Inside, a staircase, fireplace and ceiling of the original period remain. It is now the official residence of the Bishop of Bristol.

Cathedral Church of SS. Peter and Paul, Pembroke Road

The Roman Catholic Cathedral of SS. Peter and Paul serves not only Bristol but the counties of Gloucestershire, Somerset and Wiltshire.

It was designed by the Percy Thomas Partnership and consecrated in 1973. The architects designed the Cathedral with the decisions of the Second Vatican Council in mind. The interior is therefore flexible and affords a space where a congregation of 900 can easily see the High Altar and feel themselves closely involved with the celebration of the Mass.

The Cathedral is built of concrete with exterior cladding panels of brownish-pink Aberdeen granite chips. Most of the interior furnishings are contemporary and use modern materials.

The symbolic stained glass windows were designed by Henry Haig. Thousands of pieces of glass were cut to shape and set in

Christ Church, Clifton

FRANK SHIPSIDES - 1978 -

epoxy resin. The font by Simon Verity has a base of Portland stone and a bowl of Purbeck stone. The Stations of the Cross are concrete bas reliefs by William Mitchell. Mitchell also designed the entrance doors, a gift of the City and County of Bristol. These are of sculpted fibreglass and bear the coats of arms of the City of Bristol and the Bishop of Clifton.

Christ Church, Clifton Down Road

Like Holy Trinity, Hotwells, this church was built to serve the growing population of the area and consecrated in 1841. It was designed by Charles Dyer, architect of the Victoria Rooms, and added to by various architects who maintained a unity of style. It is often considered the best example of Victorian 'Early English' architecture in Bristol. The tower is by John Norton and the spire is a prominent Bristol landmark.

Clifton College, Guthrie Road

Charles Hansom designed the first buildings, the Big School, Headmaster's House and Chapel in the 1860s. Other extensions in the Gothic style were made until the 1920s.

Amongst the famous old boys of the College are Lord Roberts, British Commander in Chief in the Boer War, and Earl Haig, his counterpart in the First World War. The College has also produced writers, amongst them the novelist Sir Arthur-Quiller-Couch who edited the *Oxford Book of English Verse* and Henry Newbolt, the poet, author of *Drake's Drum*. Actors Sir Michael Redgrave, Trevor Howard and John Cleese are amongst the College's more recent old boys.

Clifton's most famous sportsman is A. E. J. Collins. Eighty years ago in a junior house match he scored 628 runs not out, still the highest recorded innings in the history of cricket.

During the Second World War the boys were evacuated to Cornwall and the buildings served as General Omar Bradley's headquarters. The College flies the American flag on July 4th each year.

Clifton Hill House, Clifton Hill

Clifton's most impressive Georgian mansion was built by Isaac Ware in 1747 for Paul Fisher, a wealthy merchant, whose monogram appears in the pediment. The main front faces south, away from the road. Inside there are some good marble fireplaces, plaster work and a superb wrought iron balustrade.

Clifton Hill House later became the family home of John Addington Symonds who achieved fame for his books on Renaissance Italy. Many of the plans for creating the University of Bristol were formulated here, and it is fitting that the mansion should now be a University hall of residence.

The Colonnade, Hotwell Road

This is all that remains of the once fashionable spa. The Colonnade was built in 1786 to meet the need for a sheltered walk. It was designed with shops below and living quarters above. Amongst the shop-keepers was Ann Yearsley, who kept a circulating library for visitors. Originally a milkmaid, she wrote poems which attracted the attention of Hannah More whose protegée she became until the poet quarrelled with her patroness. The north end of the Colonnade originally joined the Pump Room.

Cornwallis Crescent, off Granby Hill

Originally called the Lower Crescent, this row and Royal York Crescent were planned to rival the Bath crescents. Yet another casualty of the 1790s slump, it was not completed until the 19th century and the establishment of a right of way during the interval meant that the original design was not followed completely. As in several other Clifton terraces the main front faces away from the road.

Dowry Square, Chapel Row and Dowry Parade

Dowry Square and its western extension, Chapel Row, were begun about 1720. The Square was so long in building that the originally planned uniformity of style was lost. Dowry Parade was laid out about 1763 and, like Dowry Square and Chapel Row, named after the now demolished Dowry Chapel. Its houses were intended as visitors' lodgings. Humphry Davy lived at number 6, Dowry Square.

Goldney House, Clifton Hill

Built in 1720, possibly by John Wood of Bath, for Thomas Goldney, a Quaker merchant, it was badly mauled by a Victorian architect.

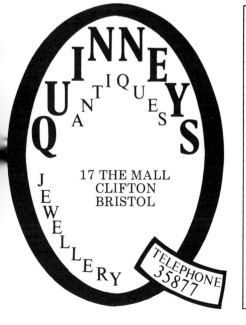

41

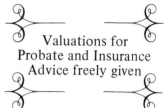

In spite of his religious faith, Goldney invested in a privateering expedition which made a large profit and which also brought back to England Alexander Selkirk, a marooned seaman, whose adventures formed the basis of Daniel Defoe's novel *Robinson Crusoe*. Goldney also backed Abraham Darby's Coalbrook Dale iron furnace in Shropshire which pioneered the use of coke smelting, and the Goldneys intermarried with the Champion family of Clifton Court.

The 18th century gardens are the most famous feature of Goldney House with an orangery, canal, Gothic garden house and tower and a bastion. The outstanding attraction is the Grotto, dating from 1739; a man-made cavern lined with minerals, Bristol diamonds and shells brought back from far shores by Goldney's merchant captains, with a smaller grotto containing a sea god fountain.

Inside the house a panelled dining room with a carved over-mantel attributed to Grinling Gibbons remains.

The house is now a hall of residence of the University of Bristol and the gardens are occasionally open to the public.

Hope Centre, Hope Chapel Hill

This former chapel was founded by Lady Hope and Lady Glenorchy in 1786 and enlarged in 1838. It followed the fashion set by the Countess of Huntingdon's Connection and had the aim of bringing salvation to the rich sinners at the Hotwells. Through local enthusiasm and effort the chapel has been converted recently into a community centre.

Holy Trinity Church, Hotwell Road

Designed by C. R. Cockerell and opened in 1830. The interior had much in common with Sir Christopher Wren's and Nicholas Hawksmoor's London churches. Bombed during the Second World War, the interior has since been re-designed.

The Mall, Clifton Club, West Mall and Caledonia Place

The Mall was originally laid out in the 1780s and is now much altered.

The *Clifton Club* was originally built as an Assembly Rooms and Hotel and opened in 1809. The architect was Francis Howard

The Paragon

Greenway who was convicted of forgery but his death sentence was commuted to transportation to Australia. Greenway was responsible for building many of Sydney's finest buildings and he is now known as the father of Australian architecture. This former forger's portrait has appeared on Australian banknotes.

Princess Victoria stayed here in 1830 when she was taken round the country and shown to her future subjects by her mother, the Duchess of Kent. The hotel wings are now shops, the Assembly Rooms are used as a gentlemen's club, and the facade has been somewhat altered.

1–13 *West Mall* and 32–44 *Caledonia Place* date from 1788, when it was originally intended to build a fourth side facing the Mall to form a square. Eventually, in the 1830s and 1840s, the two terraces were extended westwards in a different design, but one which harmonises with the earlier 18th century houses. Amongst the famous residents were Thomas Macaulay (1800–1859) historian, essayist and statesman, author of a history of England and *Lays of Ancient Rome* who lived at 16 Caledonia Place.

The Mansion House, the Promenade

The official residence of the Lord Mayor of Bristol was presented to the City and County of Bristol in 1874 by Alderman Thomas Proctor. It houses much of the civic plate and regalia. Nearby is the Merchant Venturers' Hall.

The Paragon, off Prince's Buildings

Begun in 1809 and, as in some other Clifton terraces, the front, in this case convex, faces south. The semi-circular porches with curved consoles and the blank panel above are curious in a classical terrace and foreshadow the more ornate design of the Victorian period.

Royal York Crescent

This terrace is claimed to be the longest in Europe. Building began in 1791 but the original developer, like many others, went bankrupt in 1793 and the Crescent remained unfinished until completed in 1820. During the Napoleonic Wars (1793–1815) the Government wished to convert the Crescent into barracks, a proposal supported by local brewers, but successfully opposed by

*The Victoria Rooms, a popular meeting place
and landmark since the 1840s*

46

residents. Amongst the famous residents of the Crescent were the future Empress Eugenie, wife of Napoleon III, who went to school at number 2 and the Lawrence brothers, John, Lord Lawrence (1811–1879) and Sir Henry Lawrence (1806–1857), soldiers and colonial administrators.

St Andrew's Church, Clifton Hill

St Andrew's was the parish church of Clifton until bombed during the Second World War. The tower, which escaped destruction, was demolished in 1958. The original church was built in the 12th century, extended in the 17th century and re-placed with a larger Regency Gothic church designed by James Foster in 1822. The foundations of this church are marked out at the end of the avenue of pleached limes which leads through the churchyard from the Fosseway.

St. Vincent's Priory

The Priory, opposite the Avon Gorge Hotel, is a Gothic Revival house, dating probably from the early 19th century. It is built on caves traditionally claimed to be the home of an early Christian hermit.

The Victoria Rooms, Queen's Road

The rooms were built 1839–1841 and designed by Charles Dyer who also designed Christ Church. The pediment depicting the approach of Dawn has Minerva being driven by Apollo and preceded by the Hours and Graces. Originally sphinxes stood on the forecourt but were removed at the beginning of this century and replaced by the Baroque fountain and statue of King Edward VII. The Victoria Rooms are the property of the University of Bristol, having been given by Sir G. A. Wills in 1920.

Victoria Square

The three sides of the massive Victoria Square were built at different periods and reflect the changing architectural styles.

The north east side, originally Lansdown Place, was built as a terrace on its own in the 1830's. The architects were Foster and Son, and the Foster family were with partners responsible for much major Victorian architecture in Bristol.

Royal York Crescent—Europe's longest crescent?

This terrace was followed in the late 1840s by Royal Promenade, the north west side of the Square, designed by John Foster. The round headed windows, the lively scrollwork and the arcaded attics mark a departure from the Georgian terrace.

John Foster was probably responsible for designing the south west side of the square in about 1855. The classical terrace was replaced by Italianate arched windows and the design is energetic and restless.

Windsor Terrace, off Granby Hill

William Watts, a Bristol plumber, is reputed to have dreamed a solution to the problem of making lead shot. Molten lead dropped from a tower into a bowl of water assumes a spherical shape, Watts patented the idea, which is still used, and amassed a fortune which he invested in building Windsor Terrace. The cost of raising the buttress wall bankrupted Watts in 1794 and the Terrace, which was designed to rival Camden Crescent in Bath, was completed on a reduced scale but with Royal York Crescent is perhaps the most impressive of Clifton's terraces.

Hannah More (1745–1833) dramatist and religious writer, lived at Number 4.

Zig Zag, opposite St Vincent's Rock Hotel, Sion Hill

This aptly named path is a short cut from Clifton to Hotwells. The return journey is recommended for the healthy only! Queen Victoria is reputed to have played on the path when visiting Bristol as a girl before her accession and later showed Prince Albert her playground when they returned to Bristol to launch Brunel's *s.s. Great Britain*.

Eating Out in Clifton

Clifton is fortunate to be blessed with so many fine restaurants. Between them they cater for most tastes and styles from traditional English dishes to French and Italian cuisine and international specialities. The character and style of each restaurant shows through in the imaginative and carefully prepared menus, and in the atmosphere and decor of the restaurants themselves.

The *Trattoria La Conca's* unique bar, which was built from an original wine vat, welcomes visitors and regulars to this popular Italian restaurant in Regent Street. A predominately Italian wine list, including Valpolicella wines Amarone and Barolo, complement a varied menu which has one of the Chef's specialities Veal Valdostana, a dish of veal, ham, tomato and cheese in a white wine sauce. The restaurant's lunchtime menu changes daily, offering a balanced choice in a three course, set price lunch and is available from Monday to Friday.

Mr. Pileggi had to find his car another parking place when he converted his two garages into a restaurant. The *Bon Apetit*, in Waterloo Street, is on three floors, each one so arranged to provide a comfortable atmosphere with a simple, uncomplicated decor of subtle browns and creams. Chefs prepare the principally French cuisine under the supervision of Mr. Pileggi and specialities include such dishes as Poulet Bourguignonne, chicken, diced bacon and mushrooms in a red wine sauce, and Boeuf à la Russe, thin strips of beef and mushrooms in a cream and brandy sauce.

High above the *Avon Gorge* stands the hotel of the same name. Here at lunchtime there is the choice of two restaurants, the Rib Room, where the speciality is fresh roast rib of prime Scotch Beef, and the White Lion Bar, with its self-service buffet of cold meats and various salads which can be enjoyed on the terrace overlooking the gorge and of course the Clifton Suspension Bridge. In the evening the Rib Room is open, but the buffet is only served at lunchtime. Both restaurants are, however, open seven days a week and non-residents are of course very welcome to enjoy the restaurants and the views.

Sole Cardinal, poached sole with a prawn sauce, is just one of the many fish specialities that *Rossi's* have become renowned for. Depending on the season, there are usually four or five fresh fish specialities daily including sole and salmon, in addition to their full Italian and International menu. Signore Rossi personally supervises the kitchens and cooks in this confortable and tastefully decorated restaurant to be found in Princess Victoria Street. The upstairs lounge offers an ideal setting to meet for an aperitif or to linger over a coffee after dining downstairs.

"The restaurant in town with the atmosphere of a country inn" is a description once given to the *Cauldron Restaurant* which is situated just off the Mall in Portland Street. A mixture of English and French

Georgian elegance

cuisine makes up the extensive menu available, with the choice of main courses exceeding thirty dishes. Of the many house specialities, Steak Cauldron with tomatoes, onions, mushrooms, capers and olives all in a wine and brandy sauce is just one. The restaurant's quiet, relaxing atmosphere enables the choice to be carefully considered.

The Cheshire Cat is a relaxing, friendly restaurant set in a quiet part of Clifton, Oakfield Road, where parking does not create much of a problem. Offering a small but imaginative menu, Chef uses the "Nouvelle Cuisine" method of cooking whereby all ingredients are prepared as freshly as possible and a speciality of the house is Russian Koulibiac, a salmon fish pie with prawns. An aperitif, or a pint of real ale from the wood to whet the appetite, can be enjoyed on the terrace in summer or in front of a log fire in winter. Throughout the summer, the restaurant is open Saturday lunchtime.

The Orangery is the new restaurant in the *St. Vincent Rocks Hotel* on Sion Hill. The light and airy restaurant has a panoramic view over the Avon Gorge and Brunel's Suspension Bridge, which provides an attractive setting to enjoy the varied menu. Among the Orangery specialities there can be found Clifton escalope of pork, stuffed with bacon and pate and Isambard Brunel's chicken supreme, coated in a fresh cream and pepper sauce, flavoured with sherry. A fine wine list complements the menu, and the restaurant is open for lunch and dinner, seven days a week.

The Mall shops

Downs Fitness Centre

Clifton has always been a trendsetter, so it is no coincidence that the proprietors of the recently opened Downs Fitness Centre have chosen the area to establish Bristol's first professionally staffed exercise and aerobic health clinic.

Situated in the converted Mount of Olives Pentecostal Church at the top of Blackboy Hill, and within breathing distance of Bristol's central lung, the Downs, which provide an ideal ancillary location for aerobic training, the new Fitness Centre offers a revolutionary scientific approach to everyday exercise and dietary problems.

Its focal point is a fully equipped laboratory for testing and monitoring physical fitness under the expert supervision of a highly qualified staff that includes exercise physiologists, physical education specialists and sports coaches.

On the one hand, the centre is operating as a clinic for preventive medicine, designing and administering specially prepared reconditioning programmes for the unfit, particularly the overweight business executive who faces occupational hazards through stress.

On the other, it acts as a centre of excellence, offering technical advice on all fitness training and nutritional problems, while specialising in bodybuilding and weight control for men, and slimming and figure control for ladies.

So why not join the Clifton jet set and add life to your years as well as years to your life at this pacesetting new clinic, where feeling fitter means looking better!

Mike Down, *Director*

Looking from Victoria Square into Boyces Avenue